CH

WORLD LEADERS

ANGELA MERKEL
CHANCELLOR OF GERMANY

by Edward Willett

FOCUS READERS

www.focusreaders.com

Focus Readers is distributed by North Star Editions:
sales@northstareditions.com | 888-417-0195

Produced for Focus Readers by Red Line Editorial.

Content Consultant: Peter C. Caldwell, Department of History, Rice University

Photographs ©: Maurizio Gambarini/picture-alliance/dpa/AP Images, cover, 1; golero/iStockphoto, 4–5; Peer Grimm/picture-alliance/dpa/AP Images, 7; Patrick Pleul/picture-alliance/dpa/AP Images, 8–9; Rainer Lesniewski/Shutterstock Images, 11; AP Images, 12; Globe Turner/Shutterstock Images, 15; Wolfgang Kumm/picture-alliance/dpa/AP Images, 16–17; Anticiclo/Shutterstock Images, 19; Oliver Multhaup/picture-alliance/dpa/AP Images, 20–21; Wolfgang Kumm/dpa/AP Images, 23; Sven Simon/picture-alliance/dpa/AP Images, 25; jorisvo/Shutterstock Images, 26–27; Red Line Editorial, 29; Herbert Knosowski/AP Images, 31; 360b/Shutterstock Images, 33; Chuck Kennedy/KRT/Newscom, 34–35; Noppasin/Shutterstock Images, 37; Nicole S Glass/Shutterstock Images, 38; Armin Weigel/dpa/ Shutterstock Images, 40–41; Maja Hitij/picture-alliance/dpa/AP Images, 43; AAPimages/Sight/picture-alliance/dpa/AP Images, 45

ISBN
978-1-63517-550-9 (hardcover)
978-1-63517-622-3 (paperback)
978-1-63517-766-4 (ebook pdf)
978-1-63517-694-0 (hosted ebook)

Library of Congress Control Number: 2017948127

Printed in the United States of America
Mankato, MN
November, 2017

ABOUT THE AUTHOR

Edward Willett is the award-winning author of more than 60 books. A former newspaper reporter and editor, he now lives in Saskatchewan with his wife, daughter, and Siberian cat.

TABLE OF CONTENTS

CHAPTER 1

GERMANY'S FIRST FEMALE CHANCELLOR

In September 2005, Angela Merkel arrived at a postelection debate in Berlin, Germany. Merkel was the leader of the Christian Democratic Union (CDU). She had run against Gerhard Schröder to become Germany's next chancellor. Schröder was the leader of the Social Democratic Party (SPD). He had been Germany's chancellor since 1998. The 2005 election had been close. Both Merkel and Schröder claimed victory.

The German capital of Berlin is home to more than 3.5 million people.

In Germany, there is both a chancellor and a president. The president fills a ceremonial role. The chancellor is the head of the government. To become chancellor, a leader must be elected by the German parliament, called the Bundestag.

But in the 2005 election, neither candidate's party had won a majority in the Bundestag. That meant the CDU and SPD would need to form a coalition government. In a coalition government, more than one political party shares power.

Merkel arrived at the debate at the same time as Schröder. An usher opened the door for Merkel and said, "Welcome, Mrs. Chancellor." Schröder told the usher that Merkel wasn't the chancellor. In the debate, Schröder yelled at Merkel and said his party would never negotiate with her.

As the weeks passed, the CDU and SPD failed to build coalitions with Germany's smaller parties.

△ Gerhard Schröder passed the chancellor's office on to Angela Merkel on November 22, 2005.

So, they agreed to form a coalition between the two of them. The Bundestag voted on which party leader would be chancellor. Schröder's attack on Merkel had turned public opinion against him. Merkel won. She became Germany's first female chancellor. She was also the first chancellor from the eastern part of the country.

CHAPTER 2

GROWING UP IN A DIVIDED COUNTRY

Angela Merkel was born Angela Kasner on July 17, 1954. Germany had been split in two since the end of World War II (1939–1945). West Germany had a democratic government. East Germany, however, was a **Communist** nation.

Angela was born in Hamburg, West Germany. Her father was a Lutheran pastor there. But before Angela was born, the German Evangelical Church asked Angela's father to move to East Germany.

As a young girl, Angela lived with her family in a complex of church buildings.

He was assigned to take over a small church. He went first, leaving his pregnant wife in Hamburg. When Angela was eight weeks old, she and her mother made the move as well.

The Communist government of East Germany was **atheist**. It disapproved of religion. In one instance, the government expelled students from school for belonging to a Christian youth organization. Because the Kasners were Christians, the government watched them closely.

After three years, the family moved once again. Angela's father was named head of a new school. The school was in Templin, a town in East Germany. This is where Angela grew up. She had a brother, Marcus, who was three years younger, and a sister, Irene, who was ten years younger.

Angela attended the Waldschule school, where she was an excellent student. She received straight As and often helped other students. According to her principal, Angela was particularly good at Russian, mathematics, and physics. She struggled with gym and singing.

GERMANY DIVIDED (1949–1990) ◀

East Germany
West Germany
○ Cities

TEMPLIN

HAMBURG

EAST
BERLIN

WEST
BERLIN

LEIPZIG

N
W E
S

▲ East German tanks patrolled crossing points between East and West Berlin.

When Angela was a small child, West Germans and East Germans could visit one another in the divided city of Berlin. But in 1961, the East German government closed the border between East and West Berlin. It built a wall that surrounded West Berlin. The wall separated many families. It kept East Germans from fleeing to

West Germany. Angela was only seven years old. She knew something terrible had happened.

Angela's father tried to maintain good relations with the East German government. This was difficult because the government did not trust pastors. But pastors and government leaders were both powerful. They needed each other's support to do their jobs.

Due to her father's efforts, Angela could attend university. At first, Angela wanted to study medicine. But then she decided to study physics instead. She attended Karl Marx University in Leipzig, a big city in the south of East Germany.

THINK ABOUT IT ◁

How would you feel if your city was suddenly divided in half? What if you weren't allowed to visit friends or family in the other half?

FOCUS ON GERMANY

Germany is formally known as the Federal Republic of Germany. In 2016, the nation had an estimated population of 81,762,000. The capital is Berlin, located in the northeastern part of the country.

Germany is a republic. In a republic, citizens elect leaders to govern the nation. The German government has two legislative houses, the Bundesrat and the Bundestag. The Bundestag serves as the German parliament. It has 600 members, each of whom serve four-year terms.

The official language of Germany is German. The nation has no official religion. However, Christians make up nearly 60 percent of the population. Muslims make up 4 percent. Approximately 35 percent does not practice a particular religion.

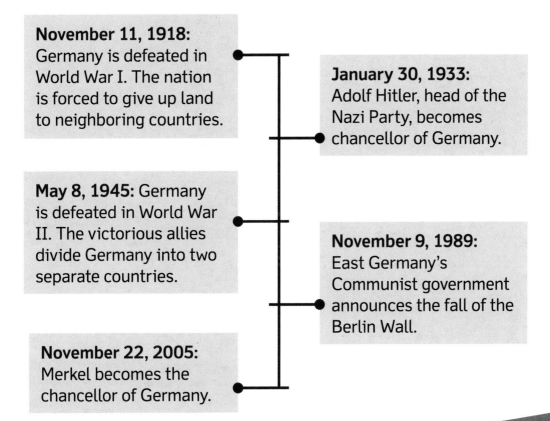

November 11, 1918: Germany is defeated in World War I. The nation is forced to give up land to neighboring countries.

January 30, 1933: Adolf Hitler, head of the Nazi Party, becomes chancellor of Germany.

May 8, 1945: Germany is defeated in World War II. The victorious allies divide Germany into two separate countries.

November 9, 1989: East Germany's Communist government announces the fall of the Berlin Wall.

November 22, 2005: Merkel becomes the chancellor of Germany.

CHAPTER 3

EDUCATION AND MARRIAGE

At university, Angela was one of seven women in a freshman physics class of 70. She began dating Ulrich Merkel, another student in the class. In 1977, the couple got married. Angela Kasner became Angela Merkel. By then, Merkel was in her final year of university. One of her papers was published in a scientific journal, *Chemical Physics*.

Around that time, the East German **secret police**, called the Stasi, were in need of members.

In August 2017, Merkel visited a former Stasi prison in Berlin.

They asked thousands of citizens to work for them. The Stasi asked Merkel, too. She would have to report what her friends and family did and said. Merkel followed advice from her father to get out of the job. She pretended she wouldn't be able to hide the job from her husband. The Stasi decided they could no longer use her.

In 1978, Merkel and her husband began working at the Academy of Sciences. This was the main research institute of East Germany. Merkel was the only woman in a group focused on quantum chemistry. During this time, Merkel and her husband drifted apart. When one traveled to conferences, the other stayed home. The couple divorced in 1982.

By the late 1970s, the government in East Germany permitted some travel to West Germany. In 1986, Merkel traveled to West Germany to

▲ Today, tourists can visit preserved sections of the Berlin Wall.

attend a cousin's wedding. During the trip, she realized the East German government wouldn't last.

Merkel was right. In October 1989, hundreds of thousands of East Germans protested in the streets. They demanded more freedom. On November 9, the East German government opened its borders. Crowds swarmed from East Berlin to West Berlin. They began knocking down the wall. Before long, Germany would be reunited.

CHAPTER 4

ENTERING POLITICS

By the end of 1989, East and West Germany were still separate countries. But the East German government was falling apart. New political parties began to form. Shortly after the fall of the Berlin Wall, Merkel joined a political party called Democratic Awakening. She left her job as a physicist to become the party's press spokesperson.

Merkel (front row, left) was elected to reunified Germany's first government cabinet.

In 1990, Democratic Awakening partnered with the German Social Union and the CDU. They formed the Alliance for Germany. The new organization wanted to combine West Germany and East Germany into one country. This process was called reunification.

In March, the Alliance for Germany won East Germany's first and only **free election**. Lothar de Maizière of the CDU was elected East Germany's new leader. De Maizière supported reunification. In May 1990, he signed a treaty that would unify East and West Germany.

Later that year, Merkel left her party for the CDU. On October 1, the East German CDU merged with the West German CDU. The next day, West Germany and East Germany were officially reunited. West Germany's chancellor, Helmut Kohl, became the chancellor of the unified nation.

Helmut Kohl (center) waves to a crowd during reunification celebrations in 1990.

Merkel met Kohl a few days before the official reunification. Kohl was impressed with Merkel's political talent. The majority of Kohl's government leaders were male. He thought a female leader would improve the government's public image.

In the first all-German election in December 1990, Merkel was elected to the Bundestag. She became the representative for a district in former East Germany. She has held that seat ever since.

In 1994, Merkel became minister of the environment. Her background as a scientist had prepared her for the role. In 1995, she led a United Nations conference in Berlin on combatting climate change. It was her first time speaking in front of a huge international audience. She thrived in the role.

In September 1998, the SPD replaced the CDU as Germany's leading party. Gerhard Schröder took over as chancellor. Meanwhile, Merkel continued to advance within the CDU. That November, she was elected secretary-general of the party. The following month she married Joachim Sauer, a chemist.

 Merkel is sworn in as the chancellor of Germany.

Despite Kohl's past support, Merkel announced in 1999 that the CDU should move on without him. Merkel's political move worked. After a financial scandal, Kohl resigned. Kohl's replacement also had to resign. Merkel took his place, becoming the first woman to lead the CDU. In 2005, after a close election, she became chancellor of Germany.

CHAPTER 5

ONE OF EUROPE'S CENTRAL LEADERS

When Merkel was elected chancellor, she became one of the leaders of the European Union (EU). The EU is a group of European countries that addresses international concerns. Merkel's party has supported European unity since the 1950s. It hoped that European countries would become wealthier by working together. Merkel also defends Europe's core principles of diversity, freedom, and **tolerance**.

As of 2017, Germany was one of 28 nations in the European Union.

As chancellor, Merkel's first major challenge was the EU budget. Each member country pays a part of the organization's budget. Merkel wanted to reduce Germany's payment. Germany was much poorer than it had been before reunification. It had taken on East Germany's weak economy.

Merkel convinced other EU countries to support a new budget. This change lowered Germany's bill significantly. Many diplomats were impressed that Merkel had achieved such a task after only one month in office.

Around the world, journalists and other political leaders took note. During Merkel's first term, *Time* magazine named her Person of the Year. Public opinion polls showed that 80 percent of Germans thought she was doing a good job.

In 2008, the EU faced a new challenge. A huge bank in the United States declared **bankruptcy**.

If the bank failed, it would hurt banks around the world. This created a global financial crisis. Governments had to step in and provide emergency funds to failing banks.

MEMBERS OF THE EUROPEAN ◄ UNION (2017)

FINLAND

NORTH SEA

SWEDEN

EST.

LATVIA

DENMARK

BALTIC SEA

LITHUANIA

Member

Candidate

IRELAND

NETHERLANDS

UNITED KINGDOM

POLAND

BEL.

GERMANY

LUX.

CZECH REP.

SLOVAKIA

NORTH ATLANTIC OCEAN

FRANCE

AUS.

HUNG.

ROMANIA

MOLDOVA

SLOV.

CRO.

SERBIA

ITALY

BULG.

BLACK SEA

MONT.

MACE.

PORT.

ALB.

SPAIN

GREECE

TURKEY

MEDITERRANEAN SEA

MALTA

CYPRUS

The crisis put many governments deeply into debt. In Greece, the government **deficit** was much higher than expected. Greece could go bankrupt. If that happened, it could drag other EU countries into bankruptcy as well. European banks held Greek loans that Greece couldn't pay off.

The EU struggled with the crisis for more than three years. In 2011, Merkel led the EU in passing the European Fiscal Compact. This treaty made it easier for the EU to deal with financial issues.

In 2015, Greece came close to bankruptcy once again. The country's leaders requested help from the EU. Merkel negotiated a tough compromise. The EU would give money to Greece but only under strict conditions. The Greek government would need to make huge spending cuts.

Not all crises during Merkel's term have been financial. In 2014, Russian president Vladimir

▲ Putin was in his second presidential term when Merkel became chancellor.

Putin ordered soldiers to take over the Crimean Peninsula. The peninsula was once part of Russia. But it had belonged to Ukraine since the 1950s. Merkel led the EU in placing **sanctions** on Russia.

Merkel has played a central role in many EU crises. Her tough-minded negotiations have earned her the reputation as Europe's most influential leader. Her reputation also makes her an important player on the global scale.

FOCUS ON
PETER ALTMAIER

Peter Altmaier is one of Angela Merkel's closest advisors. Altmaier is the head of the German Federal Chancellery. He manages how the various government departments work together. This puts him at the center of government operations.

Before Altmaier was director of the chancellery, he served as federal minister of the environment. Merkel wanted Germany to use more renewable energy resources. Altmaier became responsible for many of Germany's wind turbines.

Merkel has trusted Altmaier with other major tasks. When Greece faced bankruptcy, Altmaier pushed for German assistance. In October 2015, Merkel also put Altmaier in charge of handling Germany's **refugee** crisis.

In April 2017, Merkel asked Altmaier to write her manifesto. A manifesto is a statement of

▲ Altmaier and Merkel both work in the chancellery building in Berlin.

political goals. Merkel needed a strong manifesto to win reelection in September 2017.

German politicians were surprised with the assignment. The new task gave Altmaier even higher standing. Many Germans consider Altmaier the most powerful man in Berlin.

CHAPTER 6

DEALING WITH US PRESIDENTS

The German–US alliance has been central to both countries' **foreign policy** since the end of World War II. When Merkel became chancellor, George W. Bush was the US president. Just before meeting him, Merkel criticized US policy. She disapproved of the United States' imprisonment of terrorists in Guantánamo Bay, Cuba. Merkel showed the world that Germany would have its own thoughts on foreign policy.

Merkel and Bush discussed the Guantánamo Bay prison camp in a 2006 press conference.

Merkel and Bush had other differences, too. In 2008, Ukraine and Georgia faced threats from Russia. Bush wanted Ukraine and Georgia to join the North Atlantic Treaty Organization (NATO). But Merkel and other NATO members refused. Ukraine and Georgia had previously been part of the Soviet Union. Merkel did not want to cause conflict with Russia by protecting the countries.

Despite their differences, Bush and Merkel worked to get along. In 2006, Merkel invited Bush to her voting district. In 2007, he invited her to his Texas ranch. By the time Bush left office, Merkel felt German–US relations had never been better.

Merkel maintained her tough reputation with the United States. In 2008, Barack Obama ran for US president. He wanted to give a campaign speech at the Brandenburg Gate in Berlin. Former US president Ronald Reagan had given a famous

▲ The Brandenburg Gate is a symbol of Germany's reunification.

speech at the monument. In his speech, he urged the Soviet Union to tear down the Berlin Wall. Merkel opposed Obama's plan. She didn't want the historic gate to be used for election purposes.

Merkel's relationship with Obama improved during his presidency. But in 2013, Merkel learned that the United States was spying on Germany.

Trump greets Merkel at the White House for their first in-person meeting.

US intelligence agencies had even listened to Merkel's phone calls. Still, Merkel and Obama continued to work closely. They handled the Ukrainian crisis and EU financial crisis together.

In 2017, Donald Trump became the third US president to work with Merkel. Unlike Bush and Obama, Trump did not favor international agreements. He was focused on getting the best deal for the United States. He criticized Germany for its large **trade surplus** with the United States.

In June 2017, Trump pulled the United States out of the Paris Agreement. This was a deal between 196 countries to fight climate change. Trump thought the deal hurt the US economy. In the past, he had doubted whether climate change was real. Merkel's background in science made her a strong supporter of the agreement. She issued a statement saying she was disappointed in Trump.

Merkel met with Trump at the 2017 Group of Seven (G7) meeting in Belgium. Afterward, Merkel announced that the EU could no longer rely on the United States. Europeans, she said, had to take their fate into their own hands.

THINK ABOUT IT ◁

Do you think countries should work together or take care of themselves? Why?

CHAPTER 7

CHALLENGES CONTINUE

Germany continues to face many challenges. In 2012, wars in Syria and Iraq caused refugees from both countries to flee north. Many headed to Germany for safety.

In 2015, Merkel welcomed nearly 890,000 immigrants into Germany. Some were fleeing war. Others were in search of jobs. Merkel hoped to direct refugees away from poorer EU nations. Her East German background influenced her as well.

A group of refugees cross the Austrian–Germany border in October 2015.

She knew what it was like to be trapped in one's homeland.

Many Germans welcomed the refugees. But others were alarmed. Protestors attacked a refugee center in eastern Germany. No refugees were hurt, but 31 police officers were injured. Merkel traveled to the town and condemned the protestors. Many Germans responded. They donated clothes and toys to refugees entering the country.

Merkel's popularity fell as conflict between Germans and refugees rose. On New Year's Eve in 2015, hundreds of young women were attacked in German cities. As of July 2016, the police had identified 120 suspects. Approximately half of them were recent arrivals to Germany. Merkel condemned the assaults, but she did not change her attitude toward refugees.

▲ Citizens in Berlin rally for refugees' rights.

By September 2016, Merkel shifted her views. Parties with anti-immigrant policies were on the rise. Merkel knew she needed support to win the upcoming 2017 election. She admitted that Germany needed a stricter immigration policy.

Merkel adopted tougher laws. Immigrants faced new background checks. Officers used electronic ankle bracelets to monitor immigrants they saw as threats. Many immigrants left the country in response. Some of them left voluntarily.

Others were forced. Still, large numbers of refugees remained a challenge to the nation.

Merkel faced another major challenge in 2016. In June, the United Kingdom voted to leave the EU. Merkel disapproved of the decision. Without membership in the EU, the United Kingdom would need to work hard to maintain European relations. The refugee crisis and the United Kingdom's exit from the EU left Europe's future uncertain.

Merkel continues to act with careful boldness. According to Merkel, the German people are afraid. They fear the economy could fall. One biographer says the German people are like

> **THINK ABOUT IT**

How would you feel moving to a different country? How would it feel to not know the country's language or culture?

Merkel and British Prime Minister Theresa May discuss the United Kingdom's exit from the EU.

Merkel's children. In fact, Merkel's nickname in Germany is Mutti, German for "Mommy."

The role is only one of many in Merkel's career. The chancellor started as a small-town pastor's daughter living under Communism. Then, she became a quantum physicist. Now, she's the leader of one of the most powerful countries in Europe. In September 2017, the leader secured this position by being reelected to a fourth term.

FOCUS ON
ANGELA MERKEL

Write your answers on a separate piece of paper.

1. Write a paragraph that summarizes Merkel's rise to power, as outlined in Chapter 4.

2. How would you describe Merkel's leadership style?

3. Who was Germany's chancellor before Merkel?

    A. Helmut Kohl
    B. Peter Altmaier
    C. Gerhard Schröder

4. Why did the East German government build the Berlin Wall?

    A. to keep East Germans safe
    B. to maintain power over East Germany
    C. to start a war with West Germany

Answer key on page 48.

GLOSSARY

atheist
Lacking belief in the existence of a god or gods.

bankruptcy
The inability to pay debts due to a complete lack of money.

Communist
Belonging to a political system in which all property is owned by the government.

deficit
A situation in which more money is spent than is taken in.

foreign policy
A country's relations and interactions with other nations.

free election
An election in which voters can vote without fear or intimidation.

refugee
A person forced to leave his or her country due to war or other dangers.

sanctions
Penalties intended to force a desired effect.

secret police
A police force that enforces a government's policies, typically through spying on citizens.

tolerance
Acceptance of people whose beliefs, actions, or culture are different from one's own.

trade surplus
A situation in which a country exports more goods than it imports.

TO LEARN MORE

BOOKS

Cupp, Tonya. *Angela Merkel: First Woman Chancellor of Germany.* New York: Cavendish Square, 2015.

Throp, Claire. *Angela Merkel.* Chicago: Capstone Raintree, 2014.

Zuchora-Walske, Christine. *The Berlin Wall.* Minneapolis: Abdo Publishing, 2014.

NOTE TO EDUCATORS

Visit **www.focusreaders.com** to find lesson plans, activities, links, and other resources related to this title.

INDEX

Answer Key: 1. Answers will vary; 2. Answers will vary; 3. C; 4. B